ALL NATURAL DIET

TEAS, SMOOTHIES, BROTHS AND SOUPS THAT FIGHT DISEASES AND KEEP YOU HEALTHY

JOSEPH VEEBE

Copyright © 2017-20 by Joseph Veebe. All Rights Reserved.

No part of this publication may be reproduced, distributed, or transmitted in any form or by any means, including photocopying, recording, or other electronic or mechanical methods, or by any information storage and retrieval system without the prior written permission of the publisher, except in the case of very brief quotations embodied in critical reviews and certain other noncommercial uses permitted by copyright law.

Books in this Series:

TABLE OF CONTENTS

Table of Contents 3

Chapter 1. Introduction 7

    Introduction 7

    Ingredients used in these recipes and their health benefits 9

    Superfoods 9

    Spices 11

    Herbs 14

    Other healthy ingredients 17

Chapter 2. Wellness Drinks – Basic Drinks 21

    Wellness Drink #1: Filtered tap water 21

    Wellness Drink #2: Simple Lemon water 21

    Wellness Drink #3: Lemon water with ginger and mint 22

    Wellness Drink #4: Lemon water with cucumber and mint leaves 22

    Wellness Drink #5: Fruit infused water 23

    Wellness Drink #6: Buttermilk drink 24

    Wellness Drink #7: Ginger ale 25

    Wellness Drink #8: Hot turmeric milk 26

Chapter 3. Wellness Drinks – Teas & light drinks 27

    Wellness Drink #9: Black tea with ginger and cardamom 27

    Wellness Drink #10: Apple cider vinegar drink 28

    Wellness Drink #11: Turmeric tea with ginger 29

Wellness Drink #12: Green tea with turmeric & ginger 30

Wellness Drink #13: Masala chai (spiced tea) 31

Wellness Drink #14: Ginger and lemon tea 32

Wellness Drink #15: Garlic tea with ginger and lemon 33

Chapter 4. Wellness Drinks – Smoothies 34

Wellness Drink #16: Spicy Tropical Smoothie 35

Wellness Drink #17: Green smoothie with garlic, ginger, and turmeric 36

Wellness Drink #18: Golden yellow smoothie 37

Wellness Drink #19: Very berry smoothie 38

Wellness Drink #20: Very bitter drink 39

Wellness Drink #21: Beetroot and carrot smoothie 40

Chapter 5. Wellness Drinks - Broths 41

Wellness Drink #22: Vegan broth 41

Wellness Drink #23: Spicy Vegan broth 42

Bone Broths 44

Wellness Drink #24: Easy Bone Broth (Chicken) 48

Wellness Drink #25: Spicy Bone Broth (Chicken-Spicy) 50

Wellness Drink #26: Bone Broth (Beef) 52

Wellness Drink #27: Bone Broth (Beef - Spicy) 53

Wellness Drink #28: Bone Broth (Lamb Bones roasted) 55

Wellness Drink #29: Bone Broth (Fish) 56

Chapter 6. Wellness Drinks – Soups 58

All Natural Wellness Drinks

- **Wellness Drinks #30: Black Bean soup**......58
- **Wellness Drink #31: Lentil soup**......60
- **Wellness Drink #32: Spicy Cream of Broccoli and Kale Soup**......61

Chapter 7. Wellness Drinks – Other Drinks......63

- **Wellness Drink #33: Garlic drink with apple cider vinegar, lime, and honey**......63
- **Wellness Drink #34: Red wine and garlic**......64
- **Wellness Drink #35: Garlic and lemon drink**......65
- **Wellness Drink #36: Fenugreek Tea**......66

Chapter 8. Special conditions and recommended drinks......67

- **Cold & Flu and Fighting Infections**......67
- **Cough, Sore throat**......67
- **Nausea**......68
- **Diarrhea**......69
- **Detoxification**......70
- **Weight Loss**......71
- **Athletes Drinks**......73
- **Anti-Cancer**......73
- **Anti-diabetic**......74
- **Immune Boosting**......75
- **Anti-Inflammatory**......76
- **Reducing Cholesterol**......77

Chapter 9. Drinks to avoid or consume in moderation......78

- **Disclaimer**......80

Preview of Other Books in this Series......82

Essential Spices and Herbs: Turmeric..................82

Preventing Cancer..................83

Preventing Alzheimer's..................84

All Natural Wellness Drinks..................86

Essential Spices and Herbs: Ginger..................86

Essential Spices and Herbs: Garlic..................87

Essential Spices and Herbs: Cinnamon..................88

Anti-Cancer Curries..................88

Beginners Guide to Cooking with Spices..................89

Easy Indian Instant Pot Cookbook..................90

Fighting the Virus: How to Boost Your Body's Immune Response and Fight Virus Naturally..................90

Easy Spicy Eggs: All Natural Easy and Spicy Egg Recipes..................91

Food for the Brain..................92

Chapter 1. Introduction

Introduction

I want to thank you for purchasing the book "All Natural Wellness Drinks". The book contains a number of recipes that help boost your immune system, fight off diseases, helps weight loss, maintain your overall health and vitality. These recipes include some of the world's healthiest spices, herbs, and other superfoods. These drinks can not only fight conditions as simple as a common cold but also can keep your heart healthy, help reduce cancer risk, improve your brain function, and improve your overall health.

Water is the basic and essential ingredient to good health. More than 60% of your body consists of water. Every part of the body – each of the organs and cells – requires water to work properly. There are several benefits of water:

- Flush out toxins through urine, perspiration and bowel movement
- Lubricates joints, keeps the muscles healthy, remove cramps and sprains
- Helps maintain body temperature
- Help keep you from getting sick by flushing out toxins and improving immunity
- Proper hydration helps maintain healthy and youthful skin and promotes weight loss

The body loses water every day through urine, perspiration, and bowel movement and it needs to be replaced. Depending on body weight, health, and physical activity, the amount of water one needs vary. Typically, a person needs 3-4 liters of fluid replacement for men and about 2-3 liters for women per day. A part of this (up to 20%) comes from food and rest needs to be in the form of fluids.

By infusing nature-based nutrients (super fruits and vegetables, spices, and herbs) into the drink recipes below, we get some amazing wellness drinks that replace water loss and also nourish the body with vitamins, essential metals, anti-oxidants, and many other nutrients. These drinks not only help heal the body but also enhance the immune system in preventing many forms of diseases, help rejuvenate the body, and delay the aging process.

Some of the spices used in these recipes are tested over the ages and their health benefits are proven over thousands of years of use. Modern medicine has been increasingly studying many of these herbs and spices. By incorporating these spices and herbs along with other superfoods, in making these drinks, we get a lot more health benefits than traditional wellness drinks.

The recipes in the book are put together so that they can be easily prepared using common ingredients. There are several optional ingredients that you can try out to make the dish according to your personal taste and creativity.

INGREDIENTS USED IN THESE RECIPES AND THEIR HEALTH BENEFITS

The recipes included in this book use a combination of superfoods, healthy and medicinal spices, and herbs.

SUPERFOODS

Berries – Blackberries, Blueberries, Strawberries, Avocados

All berries are rich in antioxidants, which help neutralize free radicals in the body that usually causes cell damage. Cell damage is a pathway for many cancers and other diseases, along with aging and dementia.

The main phytochemicals in berries are called anthocyanins. These anti-oxidants can counteract, reduce, or slow down the growth of cancer cells and possibly prevent new blood vessels from forming in the cancerous cells. Berries are rich in other nutrients such as vitamin C, fiber, and minerals which can fight diseases such as Alzheimer's, Parkinson's and keep your brain sharp. Berries help in heart health, weight loss, and improve overall wellbeing.

Avocados are considered a fruit and a berry and are incredibly nutritious. Avocados have more potassium than a banana, and is heart-healthy, cholesterol-lowering and help lose weight besides all the benefits of other berries. Avocados are considered one of the brain healthy foods as it improves healthy blood flow in the brain, reduces hypertension, lowers blood pressure; all factors that help improve brain health.

Tropical fruits – Mango, Kiwi, Pineapple, Banana

Like other fruits, these tropical fruits are rich in antioxidants and many other nutrients. Tropical fruits improve mood and make you feel happier, fight cancer, protect your heart, and are good for kidneys and also provide many other benefits.

Pomegranate

Pomegranate contains powerful antioxidants called *punicalagins* which is two to three times more powerful than anti-oxidants in red wine and green tea. Other benefits of pomegranate include anti-inflammatory benefits, help fight common cancers such as prostate and breast cancers help lower the risk of heart disease, and improve brain and memory function.

Broccoli, Kale, Spinach

All cruciferous vegetables, such as broccoli, cauliflower, cabbage, and kale, are considered very good for fighting and preventing cancer. As per the American Institute for Cancer Research, they contain a compound called *sulforaphane*, which may boost the production of the body's protective enzymes and help flush out carcinogens. Besides *sulforaphane*, cruciferous vegetables also contain other cancer fighters such as *glucosinolates, crambene,* and *indole-3-carbinol*.

Broccoli is the most potent cancer fighter of all cruciferous vegetables.

Dark leafy green vegetables have been getting more and more attention lately for their health benefits. According to the American Institute of Cancer research, dark green leafy vegetables have a wide range of carotenoids such as *lutein* and *zeaxanthin*, along with saponins and flavonoids. Carotenoids prevent cancer by acting as antioxidants that lookout for potentially dangerous free radicals and neutralize them.

In addition to helping reduce the risk of cancer, these veggies are also helpful in preventing and fighting cardiovascular diseases.

SPICES

Turmeric

Turmeric has been used over several thousands of years in Asia. Curcumin, active ingredient in turmeric, has antioxidant, anti-inflammatory and anti-bacterial properties and is a key ingredient in Indian curry powder. For more on turmeric, please see my book titled "Essential Spices and Herbs: Turmeric".

Ginger

Ginger is widely used in Asian cooking and has been in use for a very long time. Ginger is extremely good for your gut which is the seat of the body's immune system. Like turmeric, ginger has antioxidant and anti-inflammatory properties as well as many other health benefits. For more on ginger, please see my book titled "Essential Spices and Herbs: Ginger".

Cinnamon

Cinnamon is also a spice used for thousands of years and is well known for its fragrance and sweetness. Used primarily in baking, cinnamon is one of the healthiest spices on earth. Cinnamon is packed with antioxidants, anti-inflammatory, anti-bacterial and anti-fungal agents. Cinnamon is good in fighting common infections due to its anti-microbial properties. Other benefits include lower and stabilize blood sugar levels in diabetes patients, lower cholesterol, and improve brain function. For more on cinnamon, please see my book titled "Essential Spices and Herbs: Cinnamon".

Garlic

Garlic is another spice that comes from the ancient world. Garlic has anti-fungal, anti-bacterial, and anti-viral properties. Garlic is good for heart health and like many others has anti-oxidant and anti-inflammatory properties. For more on garlic, please see my book titled "Essential Spices and Herbs: Garlic".

Clove

Cloves are the aromatic flower buds of an evergreen tree native of South Asia. Used extensively in Indian cuisine, clove has a history of centuries of use. Clove boosts the immune system, helps with digestion and has many other benefits

Cumin

Cumin is a spice used in the Indian subcontinent and also in other African and Mexican cuisines. Like other spices mentioned before, cumin also has a long history. Cumin has many benefits including help digestion, help with diabetes, anemia, sleep loss, and others.

Chili Peppers and Chili Powder

The active ingredient contained in chili pepper is called capsaicin which gives the pungent or hot taste. Chili pepper contains antioxidants, vitamin C, and carotenoids that provide a number of health benefits including boosting immunity, cardiovascular health, clearing nasal and chest congestion, lose weight, and treat diabetes. Chili pepper is a key component of Indian curry powder as well as many Mexican and Asian cuisine.

Cardamom

Cardamom is a spice that originated in the Indian subcontinent and is part of the ginger family. Like many other spices, cardamom is loaded with nutrients and other helpful agents that offer many health benefits from curing common colds to indigestion, lower blood pressure, improve circulation, heartburn, constipation, and many more. Cardamom is used in baking and South Asian cooking. Cardamom has a distinct taste and I always put one or two cardamom pods in my black or milk tea to enhance flavor.

Black Pepper

Black pepper is originally from South India but currently cultivated in Vietnam, Brazil, India, and other tropical countries. Black pepper has many amazing benefits including preventing cancer, relieves cold and cough, improves digestion, and many other benefits. Black pepper is also known for enhancing bioavailability whereby, it enhances the absorption of nutrients in other foods we consume. For example, adding black pepper to turmeric helps curcumin absorption by 1000 times.

Curry Powder

Curry powder is a spice mixture that is used in Indian cuisine for making "curries". The curry powder usually consists of primarily turmeric powder, chili powder, and coriander powder besides a small quantity of other spices.

HERBS

Rosemary

Rosemary is a herb of Mediterranean origin and is part of the mint family. It gives food a nice taste and aroma. Rosemary has anti-oxidant and anti-inflammatory properties and is also good for brain function, improves mood, and reduces anxiety and stress among other benefits.

Basil

Basil is part of the mint family and is used in many folk and traditional medicines in Asia. There are many varieties of basil of which holy basil is the one that has been most researched. Like many other herbs, basil has anti-bacterial, antioxidant, and anti-inflammatory capabilities. Like rosemary, basil is also a stress and anxiety reliever. Basil also has anti-cancer properties and contains many essential oils.

Cilantro

Cilantro is the leaves of the coriander plant. Cilantro is very high in vitamin A. Cilantro helps in cleaning the body of toxic heavy metals such as mercury, arsenic, lead, cadmium, and aluminum. Cilantro has anti-oxidant, anti-inflammatory properties and offers cardiovascular benefits, restful sleep, and many others.

Thyme

Thyme boosts the immune system, is anti-oxidant and helps improve circulation and protects the heart. Thyme also has anti-fungal properties and helps reduce stress.

Traditional Teas – Green Tea and Black Tea

After water, tea is the most consumed drink in the world. While the term tea has gained wider meaning in recent years, technically, tea is derived from the plant *Camellia sinensis*.

Both black tea and green tea contains several key components:

Catechins (a type of polyphenol): Anti-oxidant, anti-microbial properties

Caffeine – helps keep you alert, reduces fatigue

Amino Acids: Improves brain function, reduces stress and promote relaxation

Carotene: Anti-cancer properties

Saponin: Anti-inflammatory, anti-fungal, and anti-obesity properties

Flavonoids, Vitamins (C and E), Calcium, and Zinc.

In short, tea is a "super drink" that contains a significant amount of wellness nutrients. Tea helps to maintain a healthier heart, reduces cancer risk, lower the risk of diabetes, and improves immune function. A warm cup of tea, as you know, reduces stress, improves energy and happiness factor. Tea usually contains less caffeine than coffee.

Green tea is considered healthier than black tea as green tea does not go through the fermentation process and therefore more polyphenols are preserved in green tea.

Both teas are extremely healthy and when one adds other ingredients such as ginger, turmeric, garlic, mint, and other herbs, honey or lemon, it becomes even more beneficial as a health drink and is used as a remedy for common ailments.

OTHER HEALTHY INGREDIENTS

Olive oil & Coconut oil

Some of the included recipes use oil to roast spices before cooking or is added to smoothies. Olive and coconut oil are some of the healthiest oils. Olive oil is both anti-oxidant and anti-inflammatory, has anti-cancer properties, helps fight Alzheimer's, and is heart-healthy. Similar to olive oil, coconut oil is also heart-healthy, helps fight Alzheimer's and cancer. Coconut oil is also good for skin and hair care.

Honey

Honey is a natural sweetener, highly anti-oxidant, promotes sleep, soothes the throat, and heals burns and wounds. Honey combined with cinnamon is a good remedy for diabetes. Tea with honey and lemon is a remedy for cough.

Legumes (lentils, black beans)

Both black beans and lentils are a good source of protein. They contain fiber and folic acid and potassium which are good for heart health. They contain selenium which is good for fighting cancer.

Bitter melon or bitter gourd or bitter squash

Bitter melon is a type of tropical or subtropical vine grown vegetable primarily from Asia. Bitter melon has a long history of use in Asia – especially, China, India (Ayurvedic use), and Japan. Bitter melon is highly nutritious and medicinal. It has been used as a remedy against type 2 diabetes in many parts of Asia. Bitter melon has many benefits – some key among others include lowering blood sugar levels, improve immunity, anti-cancer properties, anti-viral, anti-bacterial properties, treat respiratory problems, and improve digestive health.

Lemon

Lemon is an excellent source of vitamin-C, an essential vitamin that improves the body's immunity. Lemon juice has many benefits including helping digestion, detoxification, promote weight loss, and balance pH levels in the body.

Apple Cider Vinegar

Apple cider vinegar has many health benefits, it promotes weight loss, lowers blood sugar and cholesterol, fights diabetes as well as cancer. Use raw unfiltered apple cider vinegar that contains "mother", or strands of protein, friendly bacteria, and enzymes. Apple cider vinegar, when used in the bone broth helps to extract the nutrients contained in the bone into the broth.

Bones (chicken, fish, beef, and lamb)

Bone broth has been used for thousands of years by our ancestors as they used every part of the animal hunted for various purposes from food to clothing to making weapons.

Lately, bone broth has gotten a lot of attention as high profile athletes and celebrities like Kobe Bryant, Gwyneth Paltrow, Salma Hayek, and many others have endorsed and incorporated bone broth as part of their regular diet regime. Bone broth has become the latest topic in the wellness world and is considered the miracle drink.

Bones contain large amounts of nutrients and minerals such as magnesium, sulfur, phosphorous, and many amino acids. The bone broth process extracts these nutrients out of the bone and into the broth so they can be easily digested and absorbed. Collagen and gelatin contained in bone broth have many benefits. Collagen is an important protein in the connectivity tissues in the human body. Loss of collagen can cause osteoporosis and skin wrinkles. Collagen and gelatin contain several important amino acids such as proline, arginine, glutamine, and glycine.

Some of the benefits of a bone broth diet:

- Improved immune system
- Healthy joints and bones
- Less joint pain

- Prevent osteoporosis
- Lose weight
- Feel younger
- Healthier and younger skin
- Healing your leaky gut
- Detoxify

Bone broth recipes included in this book combine the numerous minerals and other nutrients in the bone with the time-tested healing powers of spices and herbs. The recipes in this book are perfect for anti-aging and maintaining a youthful body and mind.

Chapter 2. Wellness Drinks – Basic Drinks

Wellness Drink #1: Filtered tap water

It is no surprise that the first thing on my list of health drinks is water.

As explained in the introductory chapter, water is essential to a healthy body. While the recommended amount of water varies with weight, height, gender and physical activity, a rule of thumb is to drink 8 tall glasses (8 oz) of water or fluid intake a day. Most commercially available bottled water is simply filtered tap water. Plastic bottles contain harmful chemicals that can seep into the water over an extended period of storage or under hot temperatures. Therefore, I recommend filtered tap water over bottled water.

Wellness Drink #2: Simple Lemon water

There are several ways of making lemon water. How much lemon juice one uses is a personal preference. Lime juice may be used instead of lemon juice. In some cases, salt or sugar is added to the lemon drink to enhance the taste.

Irrespective of how it is made (the amount of juice, lime or lemon or salt or sugar is added), lemon water is a great way to hydrate your body. Lemon water has vitamin-C and anti-oxidants. A glass of warm (or room temperature) lemon water helps in digestion and detoxification. Lemon water is also considered to be good for skin as the anti-oxidants, especially in lemon, helps in rejuvenating the skin.

Several ways to make

1. Juice (or squeeze) ½ lemon and add the juice to about 8 once (a tall cup) or water (cold or room temperature depending on preference). Mix well. This is the simplest one

2. Like in step 1 make the lemon/lime water. Add ½ teaspoon Himalayan salt (or sea salt) and mix well. This is a very refreshing drink after exercise or on a hot day.

3. As in step 1 make the lemon/lime water. Add 1-2 teaspoon brown sugar. Mix well until the sugar dissolves completely. Some people prefer sweet lemon drink.

WELLNESS DRINK #3: LEMON WATER WITH GINGER AND MINT

As in the previous recipe, make about 2 tall glasses of lemon/lime water. Crush 1 teaspoon ginger and 1 teaspoon mint leaves in a mortar. Add to the lemon water, add 1-2 teaspoon brown sugar (optional) and mix well. Strain the contents into a jug. Refrigerate until ready to serve.

WELLNESS DRINK #4: LEMON WATER WITH CUCUMBER AND MINT LEAVES

Add 1 washed and sliced cucumber, ¼ cup mint leaves, one lemon washed and sliced, one teaspoon grated ginger to 2 liters of water. Mix well and refrigerate overnight. Drink 1 cup first thing in the morning. This drink helps digestion, increased metabolism, helps rejuvenate (including skin) and nourishes and hydrates the body besides boosting immunity. Good source of vitamins A, B, and C. Due to improved metabolism, some consumers of this drink have reported weight loss after consuming this link regularly before breakfast.

WELLNESS DRINK #5: FRUIT INFUSED WATER

1. Slice a couple of strawberries and add them into a pitcher of water. Add a few mint leaves. Mix well and let it sit for 4-6 hours.

2. Wash and slice a medium orange and add it into a pitcher of water. Mix well and set aside for at least 4 hours before drinking.

3. Watermelon and herbs. Cut a cup of watermelon pieces in a pitcher of water add some herbs of your choice (mint, basil, rosemary). Set it aside for about 2-3 hours before consuming.

WELLNESS DRINK #6: BUTTERMILK DRINK

This is a well-known drink in South India, especially during summertime. In its simplest form, 1 cup buttermilk and 1 cup water are combined with one tbsp grated ginger and finely chopped jalapeño peppers (with or without seeds depending on your heat level) pulse it in a blender and add some cilantro or curry leaves and salt to taste. Below is a bit more elaborate way to make buttermilk drink

Ingredients

- 2 cups of buttermilk
- 2 cups of filtered water
- 1 teaspoon minced ginger
- ½ -1 jalapeño seeds removed and minced
- ¼ cup cilantro leaves finely chopped
- 1 teaspoon coconut (or vegetable) oil
- ½ teaspoon mustard seeds
- 1 spring curry leaves
- ½ teaspoon turmeric powder (optional)
- 1 teaspoon lemon juice (optional)
- salt to taste

Method

1. Combine buttermilk, water, lemon juice, ginger, jalapeño, and cilantro in a blender and blend for about 15 seconds.
2. Heat oil in a pan and crackle mustard seeds and add curry leaves. Add optional turmeric powder. Mix for about 30 seconds. Add it to the blended buttermilk mixture. Mix and serve.

Buttermilk drinks are common on a hot day in South India. This drink (with turmeric option) is a good remedy for cold/flu and also for hydrating during nausea or diarrhea.

Wellness Drink #7: Ginger ale

Ingredients

- 1 cup ginger, peeled and sliced
- 2-3 cups of water
- ½ -1 cup brown sugar
- 1 teaspoon freshly squeezed lemon juice

Method

1. Add ginger to boiling water and simmer it for 10-15 minutes. Stir well.
2. Add sugar and let it fully dissolve.
3. Put off the heat and let it sit until warm.
4. Strain the ginger pieces. Add lemon juice and stir. Pour the contents into a glass jar and refrigerate it.

The mixture may be used as-is (one spoon at a time) for nausea and indigestion or heartburn. You can also add 4-5 teaspoons of this mixture into a glass of club soda and drink.

WELLNESS DRINK #8: HOT TURMERIC MILK

This is an alternative version of turmeric and ginger tea (Drink #11 below) with additional spices and milk. This has all the benefits of ginger turmeric tea and more and is a common drink grandmothers and mothers make in India as a remedy for flu and cold symptoms.

Ingredients

- ½ - 2 teaspoon turmeric powder or ½ inch – 2-inch-long fresh turmeric root, sliced
- ½-1inch fresh ginger, grated or thinly sliced
- ¼ teaspoon ground cardamom (or 2-3 cardamom pods crushed)
- 1 brown sugar (or as much to sweeten to your taste)
- 1 pinch of freshly ground black pepper or pepper powder
- 1 pinch of ground cloves (or 2-3 crushed cloves - optional)
- 1-2 cups of milk of your choice (regular, coconut or almond)

Method

1. Mix turmeric, cardamom, black pepper, and cloves in a bowl.
2. Boil 1-2 cups of milk and add the turmeric mixture and mix well. Careful not to boil over.
3. Strain out any lumps if need be. Let it cool for a couple of minutes enjoy as is or add sugar and enjoy warm.

Chapter 3. Wellness Drinks – Teas & Light Drinks

The easiest way to make tea is to add a tea bag or 1-2 teaspoon loose tea into a cup of boiling water and let it infuse for 1-5 minutes depending on the tea. White and green teas require less time and black tea usually is infused 3-5 minutes. Filter out any remaining tea leaves and tea is enjoyed lukewarm. Sweetener such as sugar or honey may be added. Some add milk or lemon juice (not both together) depending on personal preference.

Wellness Drink #9: Black tea with ginger and cardamom

Ingredients:

- ½-1 inch fresh ginger, peeled and sliced/crushed
- 1 tsp honey (or as much to sweeten the tea to your taste)
- 1-2 cups of water
- 1 black tea bag
- 2 cardamom pods
- ½ teaspoon lemon juice (optional)
- ¼ tsp black pepper powder (optional)

Method

1. Add the ginger slices and cardamom to 1-2 cups of water and boil.
2. Add the black tea bag.
3. Let it cool for a couple of minutes.

4. Remove tea bag, filter ginger slices, and cardamom; add honey and enjoy warm.

You can also try the same with the addition of an optional ½ teaspoon lemon juice.

This tea is good for cold and flu. Make this tea and drink when you feel you are getting sick. Adding black pepper powder helps soothe an itchy or achy throat. If you feel like you are coming down with a fever, flu, or a sore throat, make this drink and drink it as often as you need.

WELLNESS DRINK #10: APPLE CIDER VINEGAR DRINK

Ingredients:

- 1 tablespoon apple cider vinegar (raw unfiltered)
- 2 cups of water
- ½ tbsp lime juice
- dash of cinnamon powder

Method

Mix the ingredients together and drink on an empty stomach daily. This drink helps promote weight loss, reduce cholesterol, fight diabetes and promote overall wellness.

Wellness Drink #11: Turmeric tea with ginger

This is a simple tea (does not use any regular tea bag/leaves) that contain just the wonder spices turmeric, ginger, and black pepper. This is an anti-inflammatory drink that can also provide immediate relief from cold, flu, upset stomach, or nausea.

Ingredients

- ½ - 2 teaspoon turmeric powder or ½ inch – 2 inch long fresh turmeric root, grated
- ½ inch – 1 inch fresh ginger, grated/ sliced
- 1 teaspoon honey (or as much to sweeten the tea to your taste)
- Pinch of freshly ground black pepper or pepper powder
- 1-2 cups of water

Method

1. Put the turmeric, ground pepper, and ginger in a cup or pot and add one spoon of water, mix and make it a paste.
2. Boil 1-2 cups of water and add to the turmeric & ginger paste. Mix it well.
3. Strain out the ginger/turmeric pieces. Let it cool for a couple of minutes and add honey and enjoy warm.

Wellness Drink #12: Green tea with turmeric & ginger

This is another remedy for cold and flu symptoms. Green tea has more antioxidants than regular black tea. Green tea combined with turmeric and ginger is a great combination.

Ingredients

- ½ - 2 teaspoon turmeric powder or ½ inch – 2 inch long fresh turmeric
- ½ inch – 1 inch fresh ginger grated/sliced
- 1 teaspoon honey (or as much to sweeten the tea to your taste)
- 1 pinch of freshly ground black pepper or pepper powder
- 1-2 cups of green tea.

Method

1. Process all the ingredients in a blender until smooth.
2. Add the hot green tea, mix well.
3. Filter if needed. Add honey and enjoy it.

Recipe note:

If using fresh turmeric root, either grind it as part of the rest of the ingredients or boil the root in 1-2 cups of water and green tea for 5 minutes on low heat. Then add pepper and honey once it cools down.

Wellness Drink #13: Masala chai (spiced tea)

There are several ways to make masala chai or spiced tea. When I make it, I only use ginger and cardamom. The other ingredients to add based on one's taste are cinnamon, cloves, and pepper and fennel seeds.

Ingredients

- ½ inch – 1 inch fresh peeled ginger, grated or crushed
- 4-6 cardamom, crushed
- 1 inch long cinnamon stick or ¼ tsp cinnamon powder
- 2-4 cloves (optional)
- ¼ tsp pepper powder or about 4 peppercorns
- ¼ teaspoon fennel seeds (optional)
- 2-4 tsp brown sugar (optional)
- ½ cup 2% milk
- 3 cups of water
- 2-4 tsp black tea or 2-3 tea bags

Method

1. Grind or crush cardamom, cinnamon, cloves, fennel seeds, and pepper in a spice grinder or mortar.
2. In a pan, add the ground mix and ginger and pour 3 cups of water. Mix it well and bring it to a boil.
3. Reduce heat and let it simmer for a minute or two.
4. Now add the tea, mix, and let it boil for one minute on low heat.
5. Add milk and sugar and mix well. Strain out all the ingredients and enjoy.

If you have not tried masala chai before, I suggest you start with ginger and cardamom and then introduce other items before settling on the ingredients you like best.

WELLNESS DRINK #14: GINGER AND LEMON TEA

Ingredients

- ½ inch – 1 inch fresh ginger grated or crushed
- ½ tsp lemon juice
- 1 tsp honey

Method

1. Boil 2 cups of water in a saucepan.
2. Add ginger and let it boil for 2-3 minutes.
3. Remove from heat and add lemon. Add honey once it is sufficiently cooled down. Enjoy warm.

This drink is good for nausea. Drink as often as needed.

WELLNESS DRINK #15: GARLIC TEA WITH GINGER AND LEMON

In this tea, we introduce garlic which is a very healthy spice (or vegetable, based on how you look at it) into the mix.

Ingredients

- 1-2 cloves of garlic crushed
- ½ inch fresh ginger grated or thinly sliced
- 1 tsp honey (or as much to sweeten the tea to your taste)
- 1 tsp lemon juice
- 2 cups of water
- pinch of black pepper powder (optional)

Method

1. Boil 2 cups of water and add crushed garlic and ginger and let it boil for 1 minute.
2. Add optional pepper.
3. Switch off the heat and let it sit for 20 minutes.
4. Strain out the ginger/garlic pieces. Let it cool for a couple of minutes
5. Add honey and lemon juice and enjoy warm.

This drink is good for digestion, fighting cold/flu, clearing nasal congestion and sore throat, etc.

Recipe note: Optionally 2 tsp apple cider vinegar also may be added to the boiled water along with the rest of the ingredients.

Chapter 4. Wellness Drinks – Smoothies

The smoothie recipes given below include many superfoods known for not only their nutritional value but medicinal properties as well. Many of the main ingredients such as berries, kale, and broccoli are considered superfoods that contain many disease-fighting properties. Combine these with spices and herbs such as ginger and turmeric to provide anti-oxidant and anti-inflammatory capabilities for the smoothie. These smoothies are very good for the digestive system and improve the body's immune function.

Wellness Drink #16: Spicy Tropical Smoothie

This is a tropical smoothie with a spicy twist. These fruits are rich in nutrients such as potassium, magnesium, Vitamin C, and many others. Combining them with the spices that are known to have anti-oxidant and anti-inflammatory properties, you get a great nutrient-rich and healthy smoothie. By trying out the optional ingredients and also trying different tropical fruits, one can try out different flavors depending on taste and also the availability of fruits.

Ingredients

- ½ inch – 2 inch long fresh cleaned and sliced turmeric root (start with ½ spoon and increase the amount as you develop taste for turmeric)
- ½ inch – 1 inch fresh ginger peeled
- 1 tsp honey (optional to taste)
- 1 pinch black pepper powder
- 1 banana
- 1 cup pineapple, mango or papaya
- 1 cup of milk or ½ cup plain yogurt
- ½ cup ice

Method

Process all the ingredients in a blender until smooth.

Wellness Drink #17: Green Smoothie with Garlic, Ginger, and Turmeric

A power-packed, extremely healthy smoothie that combines the goodness of greens with medicinal spices.

Ingredients

- ½ inch – 2 inch long fresh cleaned and sliced turmeric root
- ½ inch – 1 inch fresh ginger peeled
- 1 clove garlic
- 1 tsp honey (optional to taste)
- 1 pinch of freshly ground black pepper or pepper powder
- 1 cup of kale
- 1 cup spinach
- 1-2 kiwi peeled
- ½ cup blueberries
- ½ cup sliced cucumber (optional)
- ¼ avocado (optional)
- 3-4 mint leaves
- 1-2 cup filtered water (coconut water may be used as well)
- ½ cup ice

Method

Process all the ingredients in a blender until smooth. Blueberries may be substituted by blackberries depending on your liking. Serves 3-4.

By mixing and matching the "green" ingredients, you may try a couple of different green smoothies. You can substitute cucumber with broccoli.

Wellness Drink #18: Golden yellow smoothie

Coconut oil is known to have many benefits and it also helps the absorption of curcumin from turmeric.

Ingredients

- ½ - 2 spoon turmeric powder or ½ inch – 2 inch long fresh cleaned and sliced turmeric root
- ½ inch – 1 inch fresh ginger grated or thinly sliced
- 1 tsp honey (optional to taste)
- 1 tsp coconut oil
- 1 carrot washed and cut into pieces
- 1 mango peeled and sliced
- 1 cup Orange or Mango Juice
- ½ cup ice

Method

Process all the ingredients in a blender until smooth.

WELLNESS DRINK #19: VERY BERRY SMOOTHIE

Berries are superfoods with many benefits including fighting cancer, anti-aging by keeping your brain young. Fights Alzheimer's and Parkinson's.

Ingredients

- ½ inch – 1 inch fresh ginger grated or thinly sliced
- 1 tsp honey (optional to taste)
- ½ cup blueberries
- ½ cup blackberries
- ½ cup raspberries
- ½ cup strawberries
- 1 cup 2% milk or low-fat yogurt
- ½ cup ice

Method

Process all the ingredients in a blender until smooth.

Wellness Drink #20: Very bitter drink

Bitter melon or bitter gourd is an excellent natural remedy for type 2 diabetes. It is called bitter melon because it is very bitter in taste. Bitter melon is usually available in Asian stores in North America and Europe.

Ingredients

- 1 large bitter melon
- 1 medium cucumber
- ½ fresh lime
- 1 apple of your choice (Gala, Fuji)

Method

Juice all ingredients together and drink the juice daily

Recipe Notes:

1. Not appropriate for pregnant or nursing women

2. Do not combine with other diabetes medications

WELLNESS DRINK #21: BEETROOT AND CARROT SMOOTHIE

This smoothie is a potent anti-oxidant and anti-inflammatory drink. It contains vitamin A, vitamin C, vitamin E, iron, and calcium. An excellent drink when you are down with cold, flu, or want to energize yourself.

Ingredients

- 1 beetroot washed, peeled and sliced
- 2 carrots washed and cut
- 2 inch fresh turmeric root peeled
- 1 inch fresh ginger peeled
- 1 tsp lemon juice
- ½ tsp black pepper powder (optional)
- 1 cup almond milk
- 1 cup ice (optional)

Method

Put all ingredients in a blender and blend until smooth

Chapter 5. Wellness Drinks - Broths

Wellness Drink #22: Vegan broth

This is a simple broth that provides nutrition and also helps with minor ailments such as cold and flu. This is fully vegan and contains nutrients from a number of vegetables and herbs.

Ingredients

- 2-3 celery sticks cut into inch pieces
- 3 medium tomatoes chopped
- 1 bell pepper cut into pieces
- 1 large onion peeled and cut into pieces
- 1 pound (2-3 medium) carrots washed cut into pieces
- 1 cup kale
- 1 medium beetroot washed and cut into pieces
- ½ cup parsley chopped
- ½ cup cilantro chopped
- 3-4 garlic cloves crushed
- 3-4 whole cloves
- 5-6 black peppercorns or ½ tsp pepper powder
- 1-2 bay leaves
- 1 gallon water
- Salt to taste (if you must or avoid salt)

Method

1. Add everything to a large pot. Bring to a boil

2. Lower the heat, simmer covered for about 1 hr. Stir occasionally

3. Once the vegetables are cooked, strain the broth into a large bowl

4. Add salt to taste, add some chopped fresh herbs of your choice and serve warm.

5. Refrigerate any remaining broth

6. The strained vegetables are pretty good and can be eaten separately or pureed in a blender used.

WELLNESS DRINK #23: SPICY VEGAN BROTH

This is a spicy version of the vegan broth that immediately helps with congestion, cold, flu, sore throat, and other ailments due to infections. Like the non-spicy version, this broth also is nutritious and easy for your gut. The antioxidants and anti-inflammatory compounds in turmeric and ginger make this broth even healthier.

Ingredients: Veggies

- 2-3 celery sticks cut into inch pieces
- 3 medium tomatoes chopped
- 1 bell green pepper cut into pieces
- 1 red bell pepper cut into pieces
- ¼ of a medium red cabbage chopped
- 1 large onion peeled and cut into 1 inch cubes
- ½ cup chopped onion (for sautéing)
- 1 pound (2-3 medium) carrots washed cut into pieces

- 1 cup kale
- 1 medium beetroot washed and cut into pieces

Ingredients – spices and herbs
- ½ cup parsley chopped
- ½ cup cilantro chopped
- 3-4 garlic cloves crushed
- 3-4 whole cloves
- 5-6 black peppercorns or ½ tsp pepper powder
- 1-2 bay leaves
- 1 inch ginger finely chopped
- 2 tsp turmeric powder or 2 inch fresh root
- 2 jalapeño pepper sliced lengthwise (seed in or out depending on your heat tolerance)
- ½ tsp cayenne powder
- ½ tsp cumin powder
- 1 gallon water
- salt to taste (if you must or avoid salt)
- 1 tsp coconut or vegetable oil

Method

1. In a medium a pan, heat oil and add onions, crushed garlic, ginger, jalapeño peppers.

2. Sauté for 2-3 minutes or until onions become translucent. Add all the spices (cayenne, cumin, turmeric, cloves, bay leaves pepper powder) and sauté for another 2-3 minutes so the spices are blended well (make sure not to burn the spices).

3. Transfer the spice mix into a large pot (add some water to wash out any remaining spice mix from the pan and pour it into the large pot)

4. Add all the vegetables into the pot and add water, bring to a boil.
5. Lower the heat, simmer covered for about 1 hr. Stir occasionally
6. Once the vegetables are cooked, strain the broth into a large bowl
7. Add salt to taste, add some chopped fresh herbs of your choice, and serve warm.
8. Refrigerate any remaining broth

The strained out vegetables are also nutritious and may be consumed separately.

BONE BROTHS

Bone broth is considered a new age miracle drink. It is gaining popularity with athletes and celebrities as a wellness drink. By combining the immense benefits of nutrients and minerals in traditional bone broth with the medicinal properties of spices and herbs, we can make an even more potent and healthful drink. Below are some of the benefits of these spicy bone broths:

Antioxidant: Contents in bone broth such as glycine and gelatin both contain antioxidants which, coupled with antioxidants in spices such as turmeric and ginger, make bone broth one of the best sources of antioxidants. As noted in my other books, antioxidants fight free radicals (which cause cancer and other debilitating diseases).

Anti-inflammatory: By adding ginger, garlic, and turmeric in the preparation of bone broth, one enhances the anti-inflammatory properties of the broth.

Detoxification: Bone broth made by adding vegetables that contain sulfur helps the body to manufacture detox agents such as glutathione (amino acid). These detox agents help your kidneys to detox heavy metals from the body.

Bone health: Bone broth is an excellent source of calcium, magnesium and phosphorous, which help bones to stay strong and healthy.

Fight infections: As a result of enhanced immunity and a strong digestive system, bone broth helps fight infections.

Improves immunity: Minerals and amino acids in bone broth help improve the immune system.

Speedy recovery: With so many benefits such as boosting the immune system, improving the digestive system, and fighting infection, it is no wonder bone broth helps in speedy recovery of the body from common ailments.

Gut cleaning: Bone broth helps proper digestion of food and keeps your gut and digestive system healthy.

Improves joints: Bone broth contains glucosamine and chondroitin, which help to maintain joints and keep them healthy and strong.

Helps athletic performance: Healthy joints and bones help improve your athleticism and reduce joint pain after exercise.

Improves metabolism and helps weight loss: An improved digestive system and a healthy gut help promote proper metabolism and weight loss.

Beauty enhancer: Collagen in bone broth helps skin, hair, and nails to be healthy and shiny.

As you see from the above benefits, when combined with healthful vegetables and medicinal spices and herbs, bone broth indeed becomes a miracle drink that improves your health, boosts immunity, fights diseases, and keeps you feeling young.

Bone Broth Recipes

As one can imagine, the main ingredient in bone broth is some type of bone, one can mix and match additional ingredients depending on your taste, the kind of flavor you like and the level of spiciness you can tolerate. Usually, one or more of the following bones are used as part of the bone broth:

- Chicken
- Turkey
- Fish
- Beef
- Lamb or Goat
- Pork

One has a large choice of vegetables.

- Carrots

- Celery
- Tomatoes
- Bell pepper – all colors
- Beetroot
- Onions
- Kale
- Red cabbage

Spices and herbs: One or more of the following spices and herbs may be used.

- Turmeric (powder or root)
- Ginger root
- Garlic
- Bay leaves
- Whole cloves
- Black peppers
- Curry powder
- Parsley
- Cilantro
- Thyme
- Rosemary
- Oregano
- Cumin seeds or cumin powder

- Fennel seeds or fennel powder
- Cinnamon

Others:

- Lentils and beans
- Apple Cider Vinegar

WELLNESS DRINK #24: EASY BONE BROTH (CHICKEN)

This is one of the easiest ways to make bone broth. I make it out of the carcass from the rotisserie chicken bought from the departmental store. I remove all the meat and use it as a regular meal for the family and use the entire carcass (without the skins – but skins may be used as well if you prefer) for the bone broth

Ingredients

- Chicken carcass from a full rotisserie chicken – skin and fat optional
- 4 celery sticks cut into 1 inch pieces
- 3 medium tomatoes chopped
- 1 bell pepper cut into pieces (any color)
- 1 large onion peeled and quartered
- 1 pound (2-3 medium) carrots washed cut into pieces
- ½ cup parsley chopped
- ½ cup cilantro chopped
- 3-4 garlic cloves crushed
- 3-4 whole cloves

- 2 inch ginger peeled and grated
- 5-6 black peppercorns or ½ tsp pepper powder
- 1-2 bay leaves
- 1 Jalapeño pepper slit (optional)
- 1 gallon water
- Salt to taste (if you must or avoid salt)

Method

1. Add everything to a large pot. Bring to a boil
2. Lower the heat, simmer covered for about 2-3 hrs
3. Once the vegetables are fully cooked, strain the broth into a large bowl using a mesh strainer.
4. Add salt to taste, add some chopped fresh herbs of your choice, and serve warm.
5. Refrigerate any remaining broth

Recipe Notes:

1. The strained vegetables are pretty good and can be eaten after removing all the bone pieces.
2. A slow cooker or pressure cooker may be used for cooking. A pressure cooker will reduce the cooking time if you are in a hurry.
3. You can make this broth a meal by making it a soup. For making it a soup – add ½ cup split lentils, ½ cup brown or white rice to the pot. Use a mesh strainer to strain so the cooked rice and lentils pass through. Add some of the vegetables back and enjoy it especially when you are recovering from illness or

when you don't feel like having a full meal but something filling and nutritious.

WELLNESS DRINK #25: SPICY BONE BROTH (CHICKEN-SPICY)

This is a spicy version of the previous chicken bone broth. This spicy broth immediately helps with congestion, cold, flu, sore throat, and other ailments due to infections. This broth also is healing and easy for your gut besides all the long-term health benefits that come with regular consumption of these bone broth and healing spices.

Basic Ingredients:

- 4 lbs. chicken bones – any combination of wings, necks, and feet.
- 4 celery sticks cut into 1 inch pieces
- 3 medium tomatoes chopped
- 1 bell pepper cut into pieces (any color)
- 1 large onion peeled and quartered
- 1 pound (2-3 medium) carrots washed cut into pieces
- 1 gallon water
- 2 tablespoon raw unfiltered apple cider vinegar
- Salt to taste (if you must or avoid salt)

Spices & Herbs

- 2 tsp turmeric powder
- 1 tsp cumin powder or 1tsp cumin seeds
- 1 tsp coriander powder
- 1 tsp cayenne powder

- 2 tsp fenugreek seeds
- ½ cup parsley chopped
- ½ cup cilantro chopped
- ½ cup rosemary
- 3-4 garlic cloves crushed
- 3-4 whole cloves
- 2 inch ginger peeled and grated
- 5-6 black peppercorns or ½ tsp pepper powder
- 1-2 bay leaves
- 1-2 Jalapeño pepper slit (optional)

Method

1. In a medium a pan, heat oil, crackle cumin seeds, and fenugreek seeds. Add onions, crushed garlic, ginger, and jalapeño peppers

2. Sauté for 2-3 minutes or until onions become translucent. Add all the spices (cayenne, cumin, turmeric, coriander, cloves, bay leaves, and pepper powder) and saute for another 2-3 minutes so the spices are blended well and sufficiently roasted (make sure not to burn the spices).

3. Transfer the spice mix into a large pot (add some water to wash out any remaining spice mix from the pan and pour it into the large pot)

4. Add all chicken bones and vegetables into a large crock-pot and add water, apple cider vinegar and bring to a boil.

5. Lower the heat, simmer covered for 24-48 hours.

6. Once the bones and vegetables are cooked, strain the broth into a large bowl
7. Add salt to taste, add some chopped fresh herbs of your choice, and serve warm.
8. Refrigerate any remaining broth

WELLNESS DRINK #26: BONE BROTH (BEEF)

Ingredients:

- 4 lb beef bones – a mix of marrow bones, knuckle bones, short ribs
- 4 celery sticks cut into 1 inch pieces
- 3 medium tomatoes chopped
- 1 large onion peeled and quartered
- 1 pound (2-3 medium) carrots washed cut into pieces
- 3-4 beets with leaves. Leaves chopped. Beets peeled and cut into pieces
- 2 inch ginger piece peeled and grated
- 3-4 cloves of garlic
- 1 gallon water
- Salt to taste
- Pepper to taste
- ½ cup cilantro
- ½ cup parsley
- 2 tablespoon apple cider vinegar

Method

1. Add everything to a large pot. Bring to a boil

2. Using a slotted spoon, remove any foam or scum that rises to the top and continue to skim the top until the broth is clear.

3. Reduce the heat and let it simmer for one hour. Remove any remaining fat or foam rising to the top

4. Cover and simmer the broth for 18-24 hrs

5. Switch off the heat. Strain the broth into a large bowl using a mesh strainer.

6. Add salt to taste, add some chopped fresh herbs of your choice, and serve warm.

WELLNESS DRINK #27: BONE BROTH (BEEF - SPICY)

This is a spicy version of the previous beef bone broth.

Basic Ingredients:

- 4 lb beef bones – a mix of marrow bones, knuckle bones, short ribs
- 4 celery stalks cut into 1 inch pieces
- 3 medium tomatoes chopped
- 1 bell pepper cut into pieces (any color)
- 1 large onion peeled and quartered
- 1 pound (2-3 medium) carrots washed cut into pieces
- 1 gallon water
- 3 tablespoon raw unfiltered apple cider vinegar
- Salt to taste (if you must or avoid salt)
- 2 tsp coconut oil

Spices & Herbs

- 2 tsp turmeric powder
- 1 tsp cumin powder or 1tsp cumin seeds
- 1 tsp coriander powder
- 1 tsp cayenne powder
- 2 tsp fenugreek seeds
- ½ cup parsley chopped
- ½ cup cilantro chopped
- ½ cup rosemary
- 3-4 garlic cloves crushed
- 3-4 whole cloves
- 2 inch ginger peeled and grated
- 5-6 black peppercorns or ½ tsp pepper powder
- 1-2 bay leaves
- 1-2 Jalapeño pepper slit (optional)

Method

1. In a medium a pan, heat oil, crackle cumin seeds, and fenugreek seeds. Add onions, crushed garlic, ginger, and jalapeño peppers

2. Sauté for 2-3 minutes or until onions become translucent. Add all the spices (cayenne, cumin, turmeric, coriander, cloves, bay leaves, and pepper powder) and sauté for another 2-3 minutes so the spices are blended well and sufficiently roasted (make sure not to burn the spices).

3. Transfer the spice mix into a large pot (add some water to wash out any remaining spice mix from the pan and pour it into the large pot)

4. Add all chicken bones and vegetables into a large crock-pot and add water, bring to a boil.

5. Add vinegar. Lower the heat, simmer covered for 24-48 hours.

6. Once the bones and vegetables are cooked, strain the broth into a large bowl

7. Add salt to taste, add some chopped fresh herbs of your choice, and serve warm.

8. Refrigerate any remaining broth

WELLNESS DRINK #28: BONE BROTH (LAMB BONES ROASTED)

Ingredients
- 3 lb lamb bones with marrow
- 1 large onion peeled quartered
- 3 medium tomatoes chopped
- 2 carrots washed cut into 1 inch long pieces
- 2 celery stalks washed and cut into 1 inch pieces
- 1 inch ginger grated
- 3-4 garlic cloves peeled and crushed
- 2-3 tbsp apple cider vinegar
- 2 tsp thyme
- ½ cup cilantro
- ¼ cup rosemary
- 1 gallon water

- salt and pepper to taste

Method

1. Set oven to 350 degrees (176 degrees Celsius) and roast the lamb bones on a cooking sheet for about 45 minutes.

2. Add all roasted bones and vegetables and other ingredients (except vinegar salt and pepper) into a large crock-pot and add water, bring to a boil.

3. Add vinegar, lower the heat, simmer covered for 24 hours.

4. Strain the broth into a large bowl. Add salt and pepper to taste. Add some fresh herbs of your choice (optional) and enjoy.

5. Refrigerate any remaining broth

WELLNESS DRINK #29: BONE BROTH (FISH)

Unlike other bone soups, fish bone soup takes less time to make, and in many cases bones will almost dissolve into the broth especially if the bones are from small fishes. Fish bone broth is extremely popular in some of the Asian countries and carries mostly the same benefits as other bone soups.

Ingredients
- 2 pounds of fish heads and bones washed
- 3 medium tomatoes chopped
- 1 inch ginger grated
- 3-4 garlic cloves peeled and crushed
- 2-3 tsp apple cider vinegar

- ¼ cup cilantro finely chopped
- 3 quarts of water

Method

1. Put everything in a pot and add water to cover the fish heads and bones. Bring to a boil and cook for 6 hrs.
2. Strain the broth into using a fine strainer.
3. Add salt and pepper to taste. Serve warm. The broth can be used in cooking other foods as well.

Chapter 6. Wellness Drinks – Soups

Black beans are rich in protein and are one of the most healthy of the beans/lentils family. Black beans have anti-cancer properties among other benefits.

Wellness Drinks #30: Black Bean soup

Ingredients:

- 2 cups black beans – soaked in water overnight
- 1 bay leaf
- 3-4 garlic cloves peeled
- ½ medium red onion chopped
- 1 large tomato chopped
- ½ tsp pepper powder
- 1 tsp turmeric
- 1 tsp red pepper flakes
- 1 tsp cumin seeds
- ½ green or red bell pepper chopped
- 1 stick of celery cut
- 1 jalapeño (optional)
- 2-3 tsp taco seasoning
- 1 bunch cilantro

Method

1. In a heavy bottom pan, add 1 tbsp olive oil, add cumin seeds, and let it crackle.

2. Add bay leaf, garlic, onion and sauté for 1 minute and then add turmeric and pepper powder and mix well

3. Add the remaining ingredients - bell pepper, red pepper flakes, tomato, celery and sauté everything until cooked, once cooked add taco seasoning. Mix it well

4. Cook the black beans separately and set aside

5. Transfer the spice and vegetable mix into a grinder and grind it well. Transfer it into a large cooking pan

6. Now transfer the black beans along with any remaining water into the same mixer/grinder and pulse it once or twice so some of the beans are cracked or cut into halves but not fully ground

7. Transfer the pulsed black beans from the grinder into the same cooking pan, mix it well.

8. Heat the soup on a stove top until it starts boiling. No need to get it to a full boil

9. At this stage, you can add vegetable or chicken stock depending on how dilute or thick you want the soup to be

10. Switch off the heat adds the cilantro. Mix and serve warm. Rest of the soup can be refrigerated

The soup is wholesome – rich in protein and with spices and herbs is really nutritious and can be used as a substitute for a full meal, especially when you are trying to lose weight.

WELLNESS DRINK #31: LENTIL SOUP

Lentils are rich in protein and like the black bean soup from the previous recipe; the lentil soup below provides a wholesome meal especially when you are sick or recovering from sickness. These can be enjoyed as a regular meal otherwise also and is a good option when trying to eat less/lose weight and still want a nutritious meal.

Ingredients:

- 2 cups of dry lentils (any color)
- 3-4 garlic cloves peeled
- 1 medium red onion chopped
- 3 medium tomato chopped
- ½ tsp pepper powder
- 1 tsp turmeric
- ½ tsp paprika
- 1 tsp cumin seeds
- ½ green or red bell pepper
- 1 stick of celery chopped
- 1 jalapeño (optional)
- 1 tsp dried basil
- 1 bay leaf
- 1 bunch cilantro chopped
- 8 cups water/vegetable broth/chicken broth/bone broth from one of the broth recipes.
- 2 tsp olive oil

Method

1. In a soup pot, add 2 tbsp olive oil, add cumin seeds, let it crackle. Add garlic, bay leaf, basil,

onion, green / red bell pepper, pepper powder, paprika, turmeric, carrots, tomato and celery

2. Sauté everything for 2-3 minutes

3. If using a pressure cooker, transfer the spice and vegetable mix into the cooker. Add water or broth to your liking. Select chili or soup setting in an electric cooker. In a manual cooker, cook until the pressure valve lets of steam 2-3 times. If using a regular pot, cook for about 40 minutes or until the lentil is cooked well.

4. Once cooked, add the finely chopped cilantro. Add salt to taste and enjoy warm.

Wellness Drink #32: Spicy Cream of Broccoli and Kale Soup

Broccoli and Kale are considered superfoods. Combine it with ginger, garlic, and turmeric – some of the best spices and some herbs and we get a healthy and nutritious soup.

Ingredients:

- 4 cups of broccoli florets
- 2 cup of kale chopped
- 3-4 garlic cloves peeled
- 1 inch ginger peeled and chopped
- 1 medium red onion chopped
- ½ tsp pepper powder
- 1 tsp turmeric
- ½ tsp paprika
- 1 tsp cumin seeds

- 1 stick of celery chopped
- 1 jalapeño (optional)
- 1 tsp dried basil
- 1 bay leaf
- 1 bunch cilantro chopped
- 8 cups water/vegetable broth/chicken broth/bone broth from one of the broth recipes.
- 2 tsp olive oil

Method
1. In a soup pot, add 2 tbsp olive oil, add cumin seeds, let it crackle. Add garlic, bay leaf, Jalapeño, ginger, onion, mix well for 1-2 minutes
2. Add turmeric, paprika, pepper powder. Saute for another 2-3 minutes
3. Add celery, broccoli and kale and mix well so the vegetables are coated with the spice mixture. Add the desired amount of water, vegetable broth, chicken broth or bone broth.
4. Cover and simmer for 10-15 minutes or until the vegetables are cooked
5. Transfer the soup into a blender. Add more water/broth if needed. Blend until smooth
6. Return the soup from the blender into the soup pot. Heat it until it starts to boil. Mix well. Switch off heat. Add chopped cilantro, salt to taste.

Chapter 7. Wellness Drinks – Other Drinks

Wellness Drink #33: Garlic drink with apple cider vinegar, lime, and honey

Ingredients:

- 10-12 cloves of garlic (about 1 full garlic bulb), peeled
- 1 lemon
- 2 cups of water
- ¼ cup raw unfiltered apple cider vinegar
- 2-4 tsp honey or to taste

Method

1. Squeeze the cloves completely to extract juice from garlic. You should get about 2 tsp from 1 bulb of garlic. Keep separate.
2. Juice lemon and keep separate.
3. In a pan heat the 2 cups of water to lukewarm.
4. Add vinegar and garlic and lemon juice and honey. Mix well.

Consume ½ a cup 1-2 times a day and refrigerate any leftover to consume later.

This drink fights cold, flu, and other infections. Boosts immunity helps in weight loss and improves overall health.

WELLNESS DRINK #34: RED WINE AND GARLIC

Ingredients

- 1 bulb of garlic (about 10-12 cloves) peeled and chopped.
- ½ liter red wine

Method

1. Pour the wine into a glass bottle, add the chopped garlic and mix well.
2. Close the glass bottle tightly and keep it exposed to sunlight for 2 weeks (near a window possibly)
3. Shake the jar a couple of times a day to make sure the contents are mixed well.
4. After letting the mixture sit for about 2 weeks, filter the garlic out and store the wine back in a glass bottle and refrigerate.

The drink may be consumed directly 1-2 teaspoons two times a day. It can also be used as a salad dressing or for cooking.

This drink is good for cardiovascular health as both red wine and garlic have cardiovascular benefits. It has high anti-oxidants and can be used as a remedy for cold and flu.

Wellness Drink #35: Garlic and Lemon Drink

Ingredients

- 3 full garlic bulbs (about 100gm) cloves peeled and chopped.
- 4 lemons washed and chopped
- 4-5 tsp honey (optional)
- 3-4 cups of water

Method

1. Add garlic and lemons to boiling water and keep it boiling on low heat for 15 minutes.
2. Switch off the heat and let it cool down. Add honey and refrigerate in a glass jar.

Drink 3 tablespoons daily until the drink is over. Take a pause 2-3 weeks before making and consuming this again.

Recipe Note:

This is an adapted recipe from www.healthyfoodteam.com. This is a natural remedy against cancer-causing bad cells, helping to improve cholesterol and clearing clogged arteries.

Wellness Drink #36: Fenugreek Tea

This is a drink that my mom used to make for my dad. This drink has benefits in reducing cholesterol and blood sugar levels.

Ingredients

- 2 table spoons of fenugreek seeds
- 3-4 cups of water

Method

1. Roast the fenugreek seeds on low heat for about 2-3 minutes
2. Add water and bring to a boil. Cover and let it sit for 45 minutes to an hour

Drink one cup daily on an empty stomach. Refrigerate the rest. This has shown to reduce cholesterol levels.

Chapter 8. Special conditions and recommended drinks

Cold & Flu and Fighting Infections

Cold and flu usually get better over a couple of days, but the symptoms can be irritating and overwhelming. When you are suffering from flu, the key is to keep the body hydrated and also take nutrients that help boost immunity, fights symptoms, and help recover quickly. During cold and flu, the body loses more water due to sweating, running nose, etc. and so it is important to increase the fluid intake. Here are the recommended drinks for cold and flu

- Lemon water (recipe #2)
- Ginger tea with cardamom (recipe #9)
- Hot turmeric milk (recipe #8)
- Ginger and lemon teas (recipe #14 & #15)
- Spicy bone broth (recipe #25 - #27)
- Spice vegan broth (recipe #23)

Recommendation: Drink one or more of these drinks as often as needed to keep the body hydrated and boost immunity for a quick recovery. The individual taste varies so determine which of these drinks appeal to you and stick with it.

Cough, Sore throat

Sore throat and cough are usually due to viral or bacterial infections where the body's immune response results in inflammation of the mucous membranes in the throat. It causes irritation, pain when swallowing and pain in the throat while coughing. Sore throat and cough may be accompanied by chest congestion as well.

As in the case of cold or flu, it is important to take a lot of fluids to keep the body hydrated when you have a cough or sore throat. It also soothes the throat and keeps the throat membranes moist. Below are some of the suggested drinks for sore throat and cough:

- Lemon water (recipe #2)
- Ginger tea with cardamom (recipe #9)
- Hot turmeric milk (recipe #8)
- Ginger and lemon teas (recipe #14 & #15)
- Green tea with turmeric &ginger (recipe #12)
- Ginger, honey and lemon tea (recipe #14)
- Spicy bone broth (recipe #25& #27)
- Black bean soup (recipe #30)

Recommendation: Take these drinks (of your choice) warm or at room temperature. Warm drinks soothe the throat more than cold fluids. Drink as often as needed. These drinks contain immunity-boosting, anti-inflammatory, and antioxidant compounds and will help the body recover quickly. You can relieve sore throat using salt-water gargle as well. Drink as often as you need.

NAUSEA

Many things can cause nausea such as food poisoning, stomach flu, morning sickness, chemotherapy, or sheer nerves. These are all treatable with some of the drinks described in this book. In case nausea is caused by more serious ailments such as nausea accompanied by chest pain, stomach cramps, or fainting, one should immediately seek emergency medical help.

The suggested drinks for mild nausea are:

- Ginger drinks (recipe #3, #7, #9)
- Cold water
- Lemon water (recipe #2)
- Peppermint teas (off the shelf)

Recommendation: Drink as often as necessary. Make sure that you are replacing fluid loss by drinking any one of the drinks listed above.

DIARRHEA

Diarrhea is the body's defensive response to gastrointestinal issues. Diarrhea may be caused by a number of factors including but not limited to:

- Viral infection
- Bacterial infection
- Antibiotic use
- Food poisoning
- Unclean drinking water

Diarrhea in children mostly are due to viruses and be infectious. Unclean water or food poisoning can often happen when you travel across countries due to the changes in food, food preparation, cleanliness or contaminated water.

The most important thing during diarrhea is to make sure to keep the body hydrated. Dehydration (due to diarrhea or otherwise) can be fatal especially in kids and older people. Carbonated and caffeinated drinks, alcohol or milk are not advisable during diarrhea as a means of hydration. The suggested drinks are:

- Sports drinks (off the shelf)
- Lemon ginger water (drink recipe #3)
- Broth (Any of the non-spicy vegan or bone broth)
- Buttermilk drink (drink recipe #6)

DETOXIFICATION

Detox or detoxification is often used term in the healthy living context. Detoxification means flushing out excess toxins in your body. The body accumulates toxins from outside sources (foods) and inside sources (such as waste products from the normal metabolic activity). The outside toxins include chemicals from processed food such as MSG & aspartame, drugs we take for health treatment or recreational drugs, alcohol, chemicals from personal and home care products. Toxins generated inside your body include carbon dioxide, urea, and lactic acid among other things.

A detoxification regimen especially helps when one has not been eating healthy, has low energy, fatigues often, falls sick often, has aches and pains, is overweight, has bloating, or constipation often. Drinking enough water will help in eliminating waste and harmful toxins out of your body. Detoxification drinks listed here have toxin-fighting ingredients and gives the body extra ammunition to fight and eliminate toxins. These drinks usually help with symptoms associated with toxins, help boost immunity, reduce inflammation, enhance energy, and restore liver health and improve the digestive system.

The following are the recommended detox drinks:

- Lemon water (recipe #2)
- Ginger tea with cardamom (recipe #9)
- Green teas (recipe #12)
- Green Smoothie (recipe #17)
- Very berry smoothie (recipe #19)
- Lemon, cucumber and mint drink (recipe #3)
- Garlic and apple cider vinegar drink (recipe #33)
- Fruit-infused water (recipe #5)
- Ginger and lemon teas (recipe #14 & #15)
- Bone broth (recipe #24 - #28)
- Vegan broth (recipe #22-#23)

Recommendation: Individual taste and health goals vary. Once you decide which one of these drinks work best for you, drink as often as you need in small amounts between meals and in the morning.

WEIGHT LOSS

Any time your weight is more than 20% of your normal range, one should seriously consider ways to reduce weight. Obesity is one of the most significant causes of many health problems:

- Cancer

- Diabetes
- Heart disease and stroke
- High blood pressure
- Osteoarthritis
- Asthma & Sleep apnea

Unless you are underweight, keep the goal of reducing your weight every year by 5-10%. It is not a lofty or difficult goal but easily achievable by making small lifestyle changes in diet and exercise.

The following are the recommended weight loss drinks:

- Lemon water (recipe #2)
- Green teas (recipe #12)
- Lemon water with cucumber and mint (recipe #3)
- Green Smoothie (recipe #17)
- Bone broth (recipe #24 - #28)
- Vegan broth (recipe #22-#23)
- Buttermilk drink (recipe #6)
- Lemon ginger tea
- Soups (any of the soups in this book, instead of full meals)
- Smoothies (any of the smoothies, instead of full meals)
- Apple cider drink (recipe #33)
- Fruit-infused water (recipe #5)

Recommendations: Any attempt to tackle weight loss usually requires a coordinated effort of both diet and exercise. When to take weight loss drink varies depending on the drink you are planning to consume from the list above. If you are taking light drinks (lemon water, cucumber/mint/lemon water, bone broth, or apple cider drink), take one glass of your weight loss drink before breakfast in the morning on an empty stomach and another glass before lunch and one glass before dinner. If you are planning to take soups or smoothies, the recommendation is to drink the smoothie instead of breakfast or have smoothie or soup but cut down your regular breakfast, lunch, or dinner quantity.

ATHLETES DRINKS

There are two kinds of drinks that I consider athletes drinks. One is to hydrate before, during, or after the sports activity and one to maintain the condition of the body to undertake sports or athletic activity – keep the energy level and performance up, maintain healthy bones and joints, reduce inflammation and pain during or after the sports activity. For hydration, the suggestions include:

- Water (filtered tap water)
- Lemon water (recipe #2)
- Fruit-infused water (recipe #5)
- Coconut water, sports drinks (off the shelf)

For maintaining sports fitness and performance, I recommend bone broth, especially and smoothies.

ANTI-CANCER

A number of ingredients used in recipes listed in the book have anti-cancer properties. They include:

- Green tea

- Black tea
- Berries
- Broccoli
- Black beans
- Kale
- Tomatoes
- Spices – turmeric, ginger, garlic, cinnamon, and curry powder
- Herbs – thyme, basil, rosemary

This means that most drinks listed in this book have cancer fighting capabilities. Here are some recommended drinks:

- Green tea (recipe #12)
- Ginger tea (recipe #9)
- Hot turmeric milk (recipe #8)
- Very berry smoothie (recipe #19)
- Black bean soup (recipe #30)
- Green smoothie (recipe #17)

Recommendations: These drinks may be used as often as you like. The key is to use healthy; cancer-fighting ingredients to make these drinks and avoid cancer-causing foods. By making the right lifestyle choices, one can reduce the cancer risk significantly. Please read my book "Preventing Cancer" for more information on cancer prevention.

ANTI-DIABETIC

Diabetes is a condition with a hormone called insulin where either the body does not produce enough insulin or the body does not respond well to insulin. As a result, the body is not able to regulate the blood sugar level and it becomes elevated. The following drinks help fight diabetes:

- Apple cider vinegar (recipe #33)
- Masala chai (with honey)
- Green tea (recipe #12)
- Coconut water (off the shelf)
- Bitter melon juice (recipe #20)
- Fenugreek tea (recipe #36)

Recommendations: Drink these couple of times a day starting with before breakfast on an empty stomach. Bitter melon juice is the most potent of all the drinks above. Reduce processed sugar intake directly or indirectly.

IMMUNE BOOSTING

Many of the drinks listed in this book contain powerful anti-oxidants, anti-inflammatory, anti-bacterial and anti-viral properties. As such most of the drinks fall into this category. Some of the suggested drinks are

- Lemon water (recipe #2)
- Hot turmeric milk (recipe #8)
- Broths (any of the bone broths from recipe #22-#28)
- Ginger lemon tea (recipe #9)
- Green teas (recipe #9)
- Apple cider vinegar (recipe #33)
- Very berry smoothie (recipe #19)
- Beetroot and carrot smoothie (recipe #21)

ANTI-INFLAMMATORY

Inflammation plays an important role in the natural healing process in the human body. It helps to defend harmful invaders in our body such as bacteria that cause infection. Inflammation also helps the body carry out wound repair. Without inflammation, these foreign invaders could cause damage to our bodies and ultimately kill us.

While short term, controlled inflammation is beneficial, it can become a major problem when it becomes chronic, such as arthritis. Chronic inflammation plays a major role in many serious health conditions such as heart disease, cancer, Alzheimer's, and other various degenerative conditions.

Therefore, it is very important that inflammation is contained, and chronic inflammation condition is fought with either medicines, supplements or through foods or a combination of both in order to reduce or prevent it from happening.

There are a number of drinks listed in this book that help fight chronic inflammation. The suggested list includes:

- Lemon water (recipe #2)
- Green tea (recipe #9)
- Turmeric and ginger tea (recipe #12)
- Hot turmeric milk (recipe #8)
- Broths (any of the bone broths from recipe #22-#28)
- Beetroot and carrot smoothie (recipe #21)
- Very berry smoothie (recipe #19)

REDUCING CHOLESTEROL

Fenugreek tea (wellness drink recipe #36)

CHAPTER 9. DRINKS TO AVOID OR CONSUME IN MODERATION

While I have listed many wellness drink recipes, this book won't be complete unless I list some of the drinks that need to be avoided or consumed in moderation. Some of these drinks not only dehydrate the body but are also loaded with harmful chemicals and toxins that will cause long term harm to your health.

Sodas: Both diet and regular sodas contain many harmful ingredients starting with sugar, artificial sweeteners, caffeine, phosphoric acid, fructose, and others. Studies have shown a link between heavy soda-drinking with obesity and also teeth problems. Long term use of soda also can cause many other diseases including diabetes, heart diseases, and even cancer.

Sugary drinks: These contain too much sugar and are considered a major cause of the obesity epidemic.

Energy drinks: Energy drinks contain a significant amount of caffeine. Large amounts of caffeine can cause cardiovascular problems and also affect sleep, cause digestive problems, elevated blood pressure, and dehydration.

Smoothies with added sugar and chocolate: While I have listed a number of healthy smoothies, watch out for store-bought smoothies for added sugar or sugar substitutes.

Fruit Juice: While I advocate fresh fruit juice, store-bought fruit juice contains too much sugar, gone through processing and storage for a long period of time and is often artificially flavored to compensate for the natural flavor loss after long storage. The recommendation is to use fresh fruit juice whenever possible and store-bought in moderation.

Sports Drinks: While I have recommended sports drinks as a hydrating drink during diarrhea and nausea, by no means I endorse the overuse of sports drinks. Sports drinks often contain too much sugar and have added sodium both of which are not good for the teeth. Some studies have shown that sports drinks really don't rehydrate the body as much as plain water. Also, some of the electrolytes get canceled by too much sugar content.

Fancy coffee and tea drinks: Again, these fancy drinks at your favorite coffee place are loaded with sugar, calories (in some cases up to 600-800), and saturated fat. Not to mention that it is not worth the hefty cost. Avoid when possible and indulge occasionally.

Canned Soups (any canned food): Canned soups are heavily processed and are exposed potentially to toxic chemicals. To prevent the metal can from interacting with the contents, a plastic lining is usually used inside the can. This lining can cause the compounds known as BPA and PBS to seep into the soup and is a proven harmful chemical contained in most plastic bottles. This can cause cancer, type 2 diabetes, ADHD in children, and many other issues.

Alcohols: While moderate (1-2 drinks) a day is considered okay, more alcohol consumption can cause many health issues including cancer, heart diseases, liver problems, brain damage, and immune system malfunction. Besides these health problems, drinking impairs judgment, causes accidents and injuries.

DISCLAIMER

This book details the author's personal experiences in using Indian spices, the information contained in the the public domain as well as the author's opinion. The author is not licensed as a doctor, nutritionist or chef. The author is providing this book and its contents on an "as is" basis and makes no representations or warranties of any kind with respect to this book or its contents. The author disclaims all such representations and warranties, including for example warranties of merchantability and educational or medical advice for a particular purpose. In addition, the author does not represent or warrant that the information accessible via this book is accurate, complete or current. The statements made about products and services have not been evaluated by the US FDA or any equivalent organization in other countries.

The author will not be liable for damages arising out of or in connection with the use of this book or the information contained within. This is a comprehensive limitation of liability that applies to all damages of any kind, including (without limitation) compensatory; direct, indirect or consequential damages; loss of data, income or profit; loss of or damage to property and claims of third parties. It is understood that this book is not intended as a substitute for consultation with a licensed medical or a culinary professional. Before starting any lifestyle changes, it is recommended that you consult a licensed professional to ensure that you are doing what's best for your situation. The use of this book implies your acceptance of this disclaimer.

Thank You

If you enjoyed this book or found it useful, I would greatly appreciate if you could post a short review on Amazon. I read all the reviews and your feedback will help me to make this book even better. For your convenience, please click the following link to take you directly to Amazon where you can post the review.

https://www.amazon.com/dp/B07777NGGY

Preview of Other Books in this Series

Essential Spices and Herbs: Turmeric

Turmeric is truly a wonder spice. It has anti-inflammatory, anti-oxidant, anti-cancer, and anti-bacterial properties. Find out the amazing benefits of turmeric. Includes many recipes for incorporating turmeric in your daily life.

Turmeric is a spice known to man for thousands of years and has been used for cooking, food preservation, and as a natural remedy for common ailments. This book explains:

- Many health benefits of turmeric including fighting cancer, inflammation, and pain.
- Turmeric as beauty treatments - turmeric masks
- Recipes for teas, smoothies and dishes
- References and links to a number of research studies on the effectiveness of turmeric

Essential Spices and Herbs: Turmeric is a quick read and offers a lot of concise information. A great tool to have in your alternative therapies and healthy lifestyle toolbox!

PREVENTING CANCER

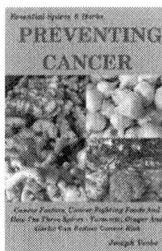

World Health Organization (WHO) estimates more than half of all cancer incidents are preventable.

Cancer is one of the most fearsome diseases to strike mankind. There has been much research into both conventional and alternative therapies for different kinds of cancers. Different cancers require different treatment options and offer a different prognosis. While there has been significant progress in recent times in cancer research towards a cure, there are none available currently. However, more than half of all cancers are likely preventable through modifications in lifestyle and diet.

Preventing Cancer offers a quick insight into cancer-causing factors, foods that fight cancer, and how the three spices, turmeric, ginger and garlic, can not only spice up your food but potentially make all your food into cancer fighting meals. While there are many other herbs and spices that help fight cancer, these three spices work together and complementarily. In addition, the medicinal value of these spices has been proven over thousands of years of use. The book includes:

- Cancer-causing factors and how to avoid them
- Top 12 cancer-fighting foods, the cancers they fight and how to incorporate them into your diet

- Cancer-fighting properties of turmeric, ginger and garlic
- Over 30 recipes including teas, smoothies and other dishes that incorporate these spices
- References and links to many research studies on the effectiveness of these spices.

PREVENTING ALZHEIMER'S

Approximately 50 million people suffer from Alzheimer's worldwide. In the U.S. alone, 5.5 million people have Alzheimer's – about 10 percent of the worldwide Alzheimer's population.

Alzheimer's disease is a progressive brain disorder that damages and eventually destroys brain cells, leading to memory loss, changes in thinking, and other brain functions. While the rate of progressive decline in brain function is slow at the onset, it gets worse with time and age. Brain function decline accelerates, and brain cells eventually die over time. While there has been significant research done to find a cure, currently there is no cure available.

Alzheimer's incidence rate in the U.S. and other western countries is significantly higher than that of the countries in the developing world. Factors such as lifestyle, diet, physical and mental activity, and social engagement play a part in the development and progression of Alzheimer's

In most cases, if you are above the age of 50, plaques and tangles associated with Alzheimer's may have already started forming in your brain. At the age of 65, you have a 10% chance of Alzheimer's and at age 80, the chances are about 50%.

With lifestyle changes, proper diet and exercise (of the mind and body), Alzheimer's is preventable.

In recent times, Alzheimer's is beginning to reach epidemic proportions. The cost of Alzheimer's to the US economy is expected to cross a trillion dollars in 10 years. It is a serious health care issue in many of the western countries as the population age and the life expectancy increase.

At this time, our understanding of what causes Alzheimer's and the ways to treat it is at its infancy. However, we know the factors that affect Alzheimer's and we can use that knowledge to prevent, delay the onset or at least slow down the rate of progression of the disease.

While this book does not present all the answers, it is an attempt to examines the factors affecting Alzheimer's and how to reduce the risk of developing Alzheimer's. A combination of diet and both mental and physical exercise is believed to help in prevention or reducing risk. The book includes:

Discussion on factors in Alzheimer's development

The list of foods that help protect the brain and boost brain health is included in the book:

Over 30 recipes including teas, smoothies, broths, and other dishes that incorporate brain-boosting foods:

References and links to several research studies on Alzheimer's and brain foods.

ALL NATURAL WELLNESS DRINKS

It contains 35 recipes for wellness drinks that include teas, smoothies, soups, and vegan & bone broths. The recipes in this book are unique and combine superfoods, medicinal spices, and herbs. These drinks are anti-cancer, anti-diabetic, ant-aging, heart healthy, anti-inflammatory, and anti-oxidant as well as promote weight loss.

By infusing nature-based nutrients (super fruits and vegetables, spices, and herbs) into drink recipes, we get some amazing wellness drinks that not only replace water loss but nourish the body with vitamins, essential metals, anti-oxidants, and many other nutrients. These drinks may be further enhanced by incorporating spices and herbs along with other superfoods. These drinks not only help heal the body but also enhance the immune system to help prevent many forms of diseases. These drinks may also help rejuvenate the body and delay the aging process. The book also includes suggested wellness drinks for common ailments.

ESSENTIAL SPICES AND HERBS: GINGER

Ginger is a spice known to man for thousands of years and has been used for cooking and as a natural remedy for common ailments. Recent studies have shown that ginger has anti-cancer, anti-inflammatory, and anti-oxidant properties. Ginger helps in reducing muscle pain and is an excellent remedy for nausea. Ginger promotes a healthy digestive system. The book details:

- Many health benefits of ginger including fighting cancer, inflammation, pain and nausea
- Remedies using ginger
- Recipes for teas, smoothies, and other dishes
- References and links to a number of research studies on the effectiveness of ginger

ESSENTIAL SPICES AND HERBS: GARLIC

Garlic is one of the worlds healthiest foods. It helps in maintaining a healthy heart, an excellent remedy for common inflections and has both anti-oxidant and anti-inflammatory properties. It is an excellent food supplement that provides some key vitamins and minerals. This book details the benefits of garlic and describes many easy recipes for incorporating garlic into the diet:

- Many health benefits of garlic including fighting cancer, inflammation, heart health and more
- Remedies using garlic
- Recipes for teas, smoothies, and other dishes
- References and links to a number of research studies on the effectiveness of garlic

ESSENTIAL SPICES AND HERBS: CINNAMON

Cinnamon is an essential spice. It has Anti-diabetic, anti-inflammatory, anti-oxidant, anti-cancer and anti-infections and neuroprotective properties. Cinnamon is a spice known to man for thousands of years and has been used for food preservation, baking, cooking, and as a natural remedy for common ailments. Recent studies have shown that cinnamon has important medicinal properties. This book explains:

- Many health benefits of cinnamon including anti-diabetic, neuroprotective and others.
- Recipes for teas, smoothies, and other dishes
- References and links to a number of research studies on the effectiveness of cinnamon

ANTI-CANCER CURRIES

It is estimated that more than 50% of the cancer incidents are preventable by changing lifestyles, controlling or avoiding cancer-causing factors, or simply eating healthy. There are several foods that are known to have anti-cancer properties either directly or indirectly. Some of these have properties that inhibit cancer cell growth while others have anti-oxidant and anti-inflammatory properties that contribute to overall health. However, many spices and herbs have direct anti-cancer properties and when one uses anti-cancer spices and herbs in cooking fresh food, there is an immense benefit to be gained. Curry dishes are cooked using many spices that have anti-oxidant, anti-inflammatory, and anti-cancer properties.

This book contains 30 curry recipes that use healthy and anti-cancer ingredients. These recipes are simple and take an average of 20-30 minutes to prepare.

BEGINNERS GUIDE TO COOKING WITH SPICES

Have you ever wondered how to cook with spices? Learn about the many benefits of spices and how to cook with them!

Find out how to start using spices as seasoning and healthy foods. Includes sample recipes,

Beginner's guide to cooking with spices is an introductory book that explains the history, various uses, and their medicinal properties and health benefits. The book details how they may be easily incorporated in everyday cooking. The book will cover the following:

- Health benefits of spices and herbs
- Spice mixes from around the world and their uses
- Tips for cooking with Spices
- Cooking Vegan with Spices
- Cooking Meat and Fish with spices

- Spiced Rice Dishes
- Spicy Soups and Broths

EASY INDIAN INSTANT POT COOKBOOK

Instant Pot or Electric Pressure Cooker is the most important cooking device in my kitchen. It saves me time, energy, and helps me prepare hassle-free Indian meals all the time.

The Easy Indian Instant Pot Meals contains includes:
- Recipes for 50 Indian dishes
- Tips for cooking with Instant Pot or any electric pressure cooker
- General tips for cooking with spices

FIGHTING THE VIRUS: HOW TO BOOST YOUR BODY'S IMMUNE RESPONSE AND FIGHT VIRUS NATURALLY

What can we do to improve our health and immune response so that our bodies are less prone to viral or bacterial infections? How can we enable our body for a speedy recovery in case of getting such infections?

The answer lies in lifestyle changes that include better hygiene

practices, exercise, sleep, and a better diet to keep our body in optimum health. This book is focused on understanding the body's immune system, factors that improve the body's immune response and some natural remedies and recipes. The book contains:
•Overview of the human immune system
•Factors affecting immune response
•Natural substances that fight viral, fungal and bacterial infections
•Recipes that may improve immunity and help speedy recovery
•Supplements that may help improve the immune system
•Scientific studies and references

EASY SPICY EGGS: ALL NATURAL EASY AND SPICY EGG RECIPES

Recipes in this book are not a collection of authentic dishes, but a spicy version of chicken recipes that are easy to make and 100% healthy and flavorful. Ingredients used are mostly natural without any preserved or processed foods.

Most of these recipes include tips and tricks to vary and adapt to your taste of spice level or make with some of the ingredients you like other than the prescribed ingredients in the recipes.

There are about 30 recipes in the book with ideas to make another 30 or even more with the suggestions and notes included with many of the recipes. Cooking does not have to be prescriptive but can be creative. I invite you to try your own variations and apply your creativity to cook dishes that are truly your own.

FOOD FOR THE BRAIN

Nature provides for foods that nourish both the body and the brain. Most often the focus of the diet is physical nourishment, - muscle building, weight loss, energy, athletic performance, and many others. Similar to foods that help the body, there are many foods that help the brain, improve memory and help slow down the aging process. While it is normal to have your physical and mental abilities somewhat slow down with age, diseases such as Alzheimer's, and Parkinson's impact these declines even more. Brain function decline accelerates, and more and more brain cells eventually die over time.

With regular exercises, strength training, practicing martial arts and other physical activities can arrest the physical decline. This book's primary focus is on managing decline in mental and brain function through diet and contains the following:
Characteristics of foods that helps in keeping your brain healthy and young. Brain healthy foods including meats, fruits, vegetables, spices, herbs, and seafood. Supplements to improve memory, cognition and support brain health
Mediterranean diet recipe ideas
DASH diet recipe ideas
Asian diet recipe ideas
Brain boosting supplements and recommendations products and dosage
References

Printed in Germany
by Amazon Distribution
GmbH, Leipzig